The Next Bezos

Your Guide To Entrepreneurship

By

Ellis Franks

Ellis Franks "The Next Bezos: Your Guide To Entrepreneurship"

This book is dedicated to all the dreamers who can see the vision and the doers who will make it all real. Every child can be whatever they choose to be, and this book is for you.

It is also dedicated to my amazingly smart niece Leah who helped me research and edit the chapters. You are already an entrepreneur at heart. I cannot wait to see what amazing things you achieve in your life.

Table of Contents

Ellis Franks "The Next Bezos: Your Guide To Entrepreneurship"

Ellis Franks "The Next Bezos: Your Guide To Entrepreneurship"

Every Kid Is An Entrepreneur

Exotic cars. Big houses. Fancy yachts. Flashy clothes. Large entourages. Millions of social media followers. Jet-setting trips around the world. None of these things represent what the life of an entrepreneur is like. The social media world promotes a culture of "fake it until you make it". This is contrary to the actual lifestyle that an entrepreneur lives. The truth is that entrepreneurship is not that glamorous. The effort it takes to be successful is not easy. It is also not an impossible thing for you to achieve for yourself at this very moment.

If you are seeking the easy life that your favorite YouTuber makes videos about then put this book down. Do not attempt to become an entrepreneur. I am not telling you this to discourage you. I am telling you this as a warning that once you start down the path of entrepreneurship all the glitz and glamour you are unrealistically expecting will no longer be the focus of your journey. Fake people will tell you that by reading this book you will instantly become rich, famous, and gain hundreds of millions of followers. This book is about the truth of entrepreneurship not fantasies. This book is a guidebook for creating your entrepreneurial habits. It is to be used as a manual for you to follow the steps required to create the entrepreneurial niche that will help you create a life that cannot be found working to build someone else's dream.

This book is not another story about a man everyone envies for his massive entrepreneurial success. His achievements have prompted a catchphrase I hear entrepreneurs use frequently when they proclaim they will "be the next Bezos" or they will "become a Bezos". These dreamers are using the well-known name as an adjective to describe the level of success they all hope to achieve. The statement "the next Bezos" means they intend on creating the next big idea that becomes a trillion-dollar business. The term describes how they expect to command the market they are entering with the same dominance as that last name demands. From this point on the term will no longer represent a single famous person. It will represent a revolution that is building in the market today where young people crave the lifestyle that they see on social media but vastly misunderstand how to achieve it. If you want to be the "next Bezos" then this book will clear up the basic misconceptions that you may have to clear your mind for the journey you will be undertaking on this path to entrepreneurship.

Ellis Franks "The Next Bezos: Your Guide To Entrepreneurship"

Entrepreneurship is vastly misunderstood by people who think the lifestyle is almost like living in a rap video. They have visions of money falling from the sky and everyone driving million-dollar exotic cars. The truth is that entrepreneurship does equal to freedom from the mundane workforce and your success ceiling is not restricted to the opinions of a boss. Success in this lifestyle is directly related to the efforts you give towards a vision of a product, service, or another concept that you created that solves a problem for others making them want to pay you for the solution.

The secret of entrepreneurial success is not found anywhere near materialistic things. People assume that success is achieved by having enough money to start to buy all the things you need. This assumption is grounded in the idea that money solves all business problems. This is also not true or every company that is making money would never fail. The history of the world's economy is littered with failed companies that produced extreme sums of money only to collapse on itself when the creators realized the business model was not sustainable.

I have walked this path for over a decade after spending nearly two decades working in an economic system that never rewarded my efforts. I learned that no

9

matter how hard I worked or how much value I created I would never gain any return on my time invested. I was paid the same or less than the person who barely skated by, then I finally had enough. I decided that I would never tie my financial future to a system that did not reward my efforts.

That is when I set forth to create my personal economy and became an entrepreneur. I was determined to take control of my future. I refused to let anyone tell me what I could or could not achieve due to their limited motivations. I would use my dissatisfaction as a personal motivator where I created millions of dollars in business by being acutely aware of opportunities when they presented themselves. I found that taking massive actions towards these prospects was important. It was also the area where most people fail.

The average person is physically capable of becoming an entrepreneur, but their limitations are most commonly found when the time comes to take actions to make the potential opportunity real. The typical response to new opportunities is fear. It nearly always causes people to freeze up at the thought of starting because the future is not known until you put action behind the concept. I have found that nearly every

Ellis Franks "The Next Bezos: Your Guide To Entrepreneurship"

person can talk about creating a better life but cannot move from being a dreamer to an entrepreneur.

Fear is not real. It is a creation in your mind that is designed to protect you in the most basic instinctual ways. The uncertainty that most people wholeheartedly believe is real is all created in your mind to keep you safe from the unknown. Entrepreneurship is the ultimate unknown because there is no roadmap for your journey because you create every step along the way. You will learn a lot of hard lessons through trial and error. Still, it is not impossible. You are highly capable of achieving anything you set your mind to doing in your life.

You are the architect of your story. Every step you take is a decision you must make on your own. Your family may serve as guides to protect you in your formative years before you are physically capable of making decisions for yourself. Then at some point in your life you will take charge of your life's decisions and become accountable for your actions. Becoming an entrepreneur at any point in your life is the same as growing up where you will take charge of the person you want to be economically. You will choose to your own decisions that will get you to your personal goals.

Ellis Franks "The Next Bezos: Your Guide To Entrepreneurship"

What Is Entrepreneurship?

I am sure that you are wondering what entrepreneurship is if it is not the glitz and glamour that Instagram makes it seem. The definition of entrepreneurship is the activity of setting up a business or businesses, taking on financial risks in the hope of profit. This is a vague explanation of the word that does not mention anything about the efforts required. It fails to mention how it is obtained. The definition also does not explain to you what steps are required to meet this goal.

I understand this dilemma because when I was very young, I never thought I could have become an entrepreneur. I assumed that only rich people could do it. There was no roadmap to success for me to follow or checklist to tick off as I went. This made the word seem like it was impossible. The reality is that becoming an entrepreneur is easily attainable for anyone. There is no law or restrictions against any person becoming an entrepreneur. If you are in certain categories there are a lot of programs that will assist you in your dream of creating something of value for yourself and the world.

My definition of entrepreneurship is formulating a concept to solve a societal problem then intelligently taking massive actions that move the idea towards a tangible system that others are willing to pay you a sum that covers your expenses plus a livable amount consistently over time. This all starts with your ability to recognize the opportunity and create a viable solution that can be profitable. The success of the concept ultimately is dependent on whether people will pay you enough for the solution to make it valuable to you.

A common mistake people make is that they do not create a real business. The wantrepreneurs end up creating a job for themselves that pays them little or nothing but requires massive amounts of effort. The misguided dreamers then become too emotionally attached to realize they have not created the freedom that is essential to truly being an entrepreneur. Entrepreneurship is the door to personal freedom at its core. It is not a leisurely activity that means you can sleep late or not work at all. If you are lazy you will fail.

Entrepreneurship is only the path for the self-disciplined. Creating your success will require a large amount of energy to build the momentum required to move your idea past the barriers to entry in your market and into a position where your business is stable. The average time this takes varies because each venture is different. You should consider that any project you begin will require anywhere from five to seven years before it becomes truly profitable.

The companies that you see commercials for on television did not magically appear overnight even though sometimes it appears that way. There is a common saying in business that every overnight success took fifteen years to create. This can be true for many opportunities that are created. You must have the stamina to stick out the tough times that you will face. It is also imperative that you have the discipline to work your venture daily to ensure its success. Consider the concept you wish to create the same as a newborn baby that requires constant attention for it to survive, only this baby may stay a newborn for five years.

Entrepreneurship is also not like winning the lottery where you will instantly receive handfuls of cash that you can "make it rain" all over town by going on spending sprees. Every cent that a new venture makes is required to be reinvested in the beginning to feed the newborn concept. Immature business owners tend to treat the revenues their business makes like it is cash flow to fuel their life. The money an entrepreneurial venture creates is not owned by the creator at this point.

14

It will be required to fuel the progress for the business as it grows. Therefore discipline is a very important trait for a successful entrepreneur to possess.

The points are not to discourage your ambition. They are to ensure you are clear what it takes to become an entrepreneur. A Greek philosopher named Heraclitus created a concept that applies to entrepreneurship where he discussed the productivity of Greek warriors in combat. His analysis was that out of every 100 soldiers, ten did not belong and would die immediately when combat began. He believed these soldiers should be killed before the battle begins because of their potential to influence doubt within the ranks. Next he stated that 80 soldiers would perform at minimum levels to hold the line but would retreat at the sight of defeat. These soldiers were looking to the best ten fighters for what they would choose to do. He believed in every battle that nine out of every 100 soldiers were the true warriors that would lead the army through their courage and their desire for victory. Most importantly, he felt the victory was truly dictated by "The One" soldier who was the champion who refused to retreat, refused to surrender, and refused to fail in their duties.

Entrepreneurship is just like this philosophical story. Out of all the posers that jump into a venture there

15

will only be "The One" out of hundreds who will be successful. The results are not because the others are not capable or competent, their failures will be because the "wantrepreneurs" did not have the discipline required to do the things that are mandatory for business success. I have heard many excuses that "wantrepreneurs" make while mentoring others. Most of them are selfish reasons that are shortsighted such as desiring to spend time with significant others, playing sports or hobbies, hanging out with friends, and any other task that diverts the attention of the wantrepreneurs from their newborn opportunities. A successful entrepreneur will be the person who sacrifices all the fun things in life today to create a life that rewards them with bigger, more important successes later in their lives. This life requires sacrifice. Conversely, it rewards intelligent work performed towards a specific goal. This balance of efforts allows means that life punishes everyone who "fakes it" along the way.

Successful Youth Entrepreneurs

Schools do not teach the skills needed to be an entrepreneur. The basic education that is received over the thirteen years each of us is forced to attend does a poor job to create an entrepreneurial spirit. The lessons taught are to follow the rules, meet deadlines, researching, and completing projects. Very few classes teach useable skills that an entrepreneur will need to be

16

successful. It is your personal responsibility to seek role models and mentors that you can use as positive examples that you can use as guides to meet your goals.

Role models are sometimes hard to determine because social media culture promotes people who do outrageous things. It gives little attention to people who are positive influences. The amount of "likes", "follows", or "retweets" is not the value of a role model. The content that is viral many times lacks the core values that will help you become successful. Therefore your social media feeds are saturated with all your friends posing in the same pose that Kylie Jenner posted months earlier because it has now become a trend on the platforms.

Role models should be studied based on their positive influences and the value of their content to make your life better. It will take some adjusting to see true valuable content versus just popular garbage on social media. Once you can identify the traits a role model should have then you can seek those types of people to follow. You must understand that entrepreneurs are not followers. The personality types that are the most successful in this world are the ones that separate themselves from the pack to create their own viral waves of success.

17

My guideline for picking a role model is first based on the value of their content. If you cannot gain useful bits of information about how the influencer made it to their level then they are not helping you. If the message they send out to the world is not positive then they will pull you down into their negativity. A true role model will display a passion for helping others achieve greatness over all things.

I purged all the negative influences out of my life when I began my leadership journey in 2001. When I conducted an audit of my role models I found only negative influencers that were not helping me grow as a leader. I was listening to mostly rap music, watching a lot of television, and hanging out with people who did not build me up to make me better. I made a personal decision to eliminate these poor influencers which ended up changing my life forever.

I replaced the things I put into my mind with positive ones that gave me positive steps to take to be successful. I stopped hanging out with the crowd of people whose only ambition was to party every day. I audited the chain of leaders above me seeking role models only to find I would be required to look outside of my career field to find positive ones. These changes were the beginning of my successful journey to becoming an entrepreneur, but the changes were not immediate. It required dedication to changing daily.

If you are in a situation where you feel there are no positive role models to choose from then seek them outside of your current circle. There are amazing people in every community who would love to mentor a young superstar if you seek them out. Mentors also do not have to be physically present to mentor you because of the abundance of digital media options at your fingertips. You can download books from people you admire to study their success habits. This is mentorship.

Mentors, like myself, write these books to affect change in the largest number of people possible by telling you the insights we learned the hard way in our own journeys. I was mentoring business owners one at a time affecting small changes in people's lives when I decided I would write books about the things I wished I knew when I started. My goal in writing any book is to give you a starting point far ahead of where I started. This is the type of mentorship you should seek. I am a mentor to you through my words. I recommend that you learn from a diverse group of mentors to ensure that you receive a the most well-rounded entrepreneurial education possible. Then after succeeding I challenge

19

you to pay it forward by writing your own book about your journey to help others from similar backgrounds like yours.

I believe selecting proper roles models is the most important decision you will make in your life. The choice of these mentors will influence how your entrepreneurial character develops. The choice of mentors is diverse so you should consider picking the role models that mirror your personality at first. The ideas are to make the transition easier because the traits of each can be easier to adapt when they fit your personality quirks. After you are more seasoned I challenge you to open your mind to new voices of influence to expand your understanding of success. This will also help you grow as a person when you learn from diverse people or cultures.

The entrepreneurs we highlight here are youth who are uber motivated to be successful. Their stories are as different as the products they created. We had to narrow down our research list to three from dozens of equally exceptional young entrepreneurs and the ones we chose to discuss are George Matus (Teal Drones), Brandon and Sebastian Martinez (Are You Kidding), and Maya Penn (Maya's Ideas). These three entrepreneurial stories spoke to us as excellent role models for everyone to study how they became successful in their markets.

GEORGE MATUS, CEO

"This company; this drone; they really just started from my own love of flying."

George Matus started "Teal Drones" when he was just 18 years old. He started building drones well before he launched his company. He is credited with creating the world's fastest production drone. His accomplishments also include being recognized on the Forbes 30 Under 30 list and being selected as a Thiel Fellow. These accomplishments are exceptional considering he is only 20 years old.

Matus is now competing for an Department of Defense contract to supply the US Army with enhanced drone technologies that is worth over $100 million. His company is a favorite in the race to upgrade the current drone capabilities because his early models were highly customizable which is something that the Army prizes. The success of his business lies with his love for the industry he is helping to build.

21

The value of Matus' story is found in the passion he has for flying. He was an avid radio-controlled enthusiast. His desire to build models to fly outpaced the state of the industry. He decided that instead of waiting on someone else to build the technology he would take the initiative to create his own flying models. This led him to creating his first drones and essentially the creation of his business years later.

Matus shows you that you can follow your passions to create something special if you have the courage to take the first step. This pivotal quality is the difference between being a dreamer who talks about being successful and becoming the next successful youth entrepreneur. His story should be an example for you to follow your passions to create your own path to success.

Brandon & Sebastian Martinez, Founders

"You're never too old or too young to start a business... you can be 7 or 70."- Sebastian Martinez

Brandon and Sebastian Martinez started sock company "Are You Kidding". The business grew from the duos love for being different. They wanted to create fun designs for the socks they wore. This led them to

22

start selling their creations online. Their products were a hit with their target audience.

The brothers started out with a love for creating unique socks designs but quickly adapted a more important purpose for their business. They decided to develop a cause-based business model where they used profits to help also raise money for charitable causes. The list of causes they have supported include Live Like Bella, Special Olympics, Big Brother Big Sister, Make-A-Wish Foundation, and other organizations they feel are important.

The most important factor to the brothers' success is that their mother recognized the passion that young Sebastian had for socks then set forth to create their family business. Her support was the influence that moved Sebastian's passion towards the reality of creating the successful venture. Behind every successful business you will find someone like their mother who helped the vision become a reality. If you do not have immediate family who can help you then you must find outside mentorship to help you open the doors required to start a business.

Sebastian is now an 11-year-old CEO of a successful cause-based brand. His success can be found in his passion for what he has created. It is also important to understand that his success is very much tied to his desire to help others. This is a trait that all young entrepreneurs should follow because true success always lies in helping others.

Brandon is now a 13-year-old Director of Sales for their brand. His support for his brother's dream is very honorable. He displays the core value of service before self because he is not jealous of his brother being "the boss". He shows an extreme maturity that all entrepreneurs can learn from to grow as business owners because he shows true humility in his role with the company. He understands that their mission is more important than individual successes making their partnership a success.

Maya Penn, CEO

"Everyone starts small…it takes a lot of hard work"

Maya Penn founded Maya's Ideas in 2008 when she was 8 years old. She created a business that sells environmentally sustainable fashion accessories. Her rise to fame is notable as she has been recognized by

24

many influencers, such as Oprah Winfrey, as a business savant earning her a multitude of high-level awards.

Maya has already been a force in business for over a decade at age 19. She is a highly sought-after keynote speaker for the world's largest companies as she always delivers a fresh perspective on business, life, and her passion for curbing environmental pollution. Her efforts also earned her a commendation from President Barack Obama for her influences on environmental stewardship.

Maya has also written books to help other people be successful. Her book "You Got This" details her amazing journey to becoming a major influencer in the world. It is an excellent guide for all young entrepreneurs to use to tap into the drive that makes her successful. I recommend this book for you to use her as an external mentor because Maya has star power that you can follow if you take her lessons to heart.

These stories are just a few about the amazing youth entrepreneurs we have today. For every Maya there is another young entrepreneur who is not as well-known but is still as successful in their own ventures. These are the types of role models you must follow to be

25

successful. You will not find these successful youth spending hours playing Fortnite because they are engaged in passions that are rewarding them, not distracting them from their purpose.

I challenge you to seek out more successful youth then use their stories to fuel your own journey. You can only be successful following proper role models. The fakers on Instagram will try to show you they are rich and famous for doing nothing other than posting pictures of their lives. This is not a reality. These people are trying to fool the world into making them important while they provide nothing of value to the world.

The difference in George Matus, Sebastian & Brandon Martinez, Maya Penn, and the fakers on social media are that these very successful young entrepreneurs are creating value for their markets. They are also creating awareness for the causes they believe are important. They do this not with random pics of the same poses twenty times a day, but with solving problems they see in their own lives.

This is the lesson you must take to heart. If you want to be successful you must follow their leads by looking up from the iPhone screen to see the problems around you. Then when they are identified you must take actions. Each of the highlighted entrepreneurs saw the same deficiencies in the markets they entered, but instead of posting negative comments about it all they created a business to solve it. You cannot see opportunity refreshing your social media feeds. You must find your passion then pour all that energy into making it successful. Successful entrepreneurs are doers first then enjoy the fruits of their labors later.

We call this "The Law of The Price Tag" in leadership training. The law was created by the world's leading leadership guru John C. Maxwell. He stated that you must always "pay now" or you will "pay later" with failure. This means that success is found after you have paid the price of overcoming all the barriers that have made other people give up on fixing the problem you have identified. Once the barriers have been overcome then you will have earned the right to "live your best life" as the fakers claim they do on social media.

Common Misbeliefs

The entrepreneur world is full of misbeliefs that are spread by people who more than likely are not truly entrepreneurs. Most entrepreneurs are too busy to be out making bold claims about the lives they lead because success requires a laser-focused approach. I will discuss

27

a few of the most common misbeliefs I have heard to give you the truest answer possible based on real experiences.

The first misbelief I hear from people is that entrepreneurs are born a certain way. This is not true. Entrepreneurs will possess similar values, traits, and work ethics but this does not mean they were born with innate qualities that make them better than others. I was born into a low-income family with no opportunities, no support, and drug culture influences all around me. I made personal choices on my journey that separated me from those negative influences to position myself to be successful.

You will be required to make these choices on your journey at some point. The difference between success or failure will be determined by your business discipline. This means if you have the discipline to remain on task when presented with other opportunities to engage in distractions then you will find success more often than failure. The key trait to the decision made will be decided by your personal discipline.

Discipline is a choice, not an innate factor to determine your success. This means that you control

28

your decisions as well as the choices that lead to other outcomes. Having consistency in discipline will ensure more positive results for a young entrepreneur than someone who is not disciplined.

This means that success is a choice. It is not the path you were just born to do. Success is the result of being disciplined long enough in your venture to reap the benefits of your intelligent, hard work. Each person does have innate talents, varying intelligence, and other innate factors that enhance the value they can bring. These are not the factors that create success. These are the tools that give each person their own skills to earn their success in their own way.

The way to enhance your success is to understand your strengths and weaknesses to better understand where to spend your time learning skills. You should rely on your innate talents like a Jedi used the force, where the skills you have enhance your physical abilities. This does not mean you are defined by the innate talents you were gifted. It means that you must spend time learning in areas you are not naturally gifted.

The story of St. Louis Cardinals former pitcher Rick Ankiel shows this very lesson. Rick was a

29

dominate pitcher when he made his way to the Major Leagues in 1999. He had earned awards at every level he played from high school through the pros as a pitcher.

Then one day Rick forgot how to pitch. His command of the baseball was lost in what seemed like an instant. Pitchers who cannot pitch quickly find themselves jobless. Rick looked like he was done playing professional baseball because most pitchers focus on their strengths only. Pitchers are rarely good hitters because they do not focus on the skills required to be successful at the Major League level.

Rick was different. He was a good hitter for a pitcher. He took the time required to prepare for games taking batting practice when other pitchers would skip it. Rick was at a major crossroads in his career. If he decided to only be a pitcher then he was done. He then decided to lobby the Cardinals organization for him to be converted to an outfielder. The Cardinals agreed to his demand with a slight change in the plans. Rick would be sent back down to the minor leagues to prove himself all over again.

The life a Major League baseball player lives is very different than what is experienced in the minors.

30

An established player like Rick usually lacks the humility required to make the transition from the top level to a complete restart. He made the decision to go for it. In the end his consistent work on his weak areas preparing for his pitching starts led to him remaining a Major League player for several more years. His discipline and consistency of his character was a contributing factor in him playing at the highest level for six separate teams. He was born a pitcher but retired an outfielder after 14 years.

No matter your innate talents you can train yourself, just like Rick Ankiel did for his position, to be an entrepreneur. No one is born to be anything, they choose to be, or they accept whatever they are given. This is a choice not a divined path. If you want it then prepare.

The next misbelief that is spread as an absolute truth is that creating some brilliant idea will make you an instant entrepreneur. Yes, entrepreneurship requires the formulation of a solution to a problem. This is better known as an idea, but it is not the finishing point for creating an entrepreneurial venture.

Most people know who Thomas Edison is or at a minimum are familiar with the things he created. Edison is most known for being the inventor of the light bulb. His idea is still used today over the entire planet. This was not his most successful creation. He invented the phonograph as well having the creation widely sought after by the masses. The problem was that Edison was very good at creating ideas, but lacked the discipline required to be a successful entrepreneur.

Edison patented 1,093 designs for ideas he had. Still when he died he was mostly broke. His ability to see concepts that did not exist was very high. His weakness was that he did not have the discipline required to take the idea from concept to sustainment in the market. Edison only wanted to invent new things then get paid, but this is not how business works. The success of an idea is mainly tied to the efforts the creator places behind it. Edison would end up having his phonograph design being improved upon because he had already moved onto the next idea. This caused him financial loss because he had received royalties from his invention until it had become obsolete by a better design. If Edison was more disciplined in terms of his business acumen then today we possibly would have called him the father of modern media. This thought is because had he focused on his most successful business creation he would have undoubtedly pushed that segment of

32

technology to the highest levels of possibility during his lifetime. He also would possible have become extremely wealthy in the process, but he chose a different path where he created many inventions that pushed numerous industries forward. His decision gained him legendary status, but he died the ward of his wealthy benefactor Henry Ford.

Ideas do not guarantee success. If this were true then universities would be staffed by the wealthiest people in the world because they are constantly creating new concepts that would gain them instant riches. In case you missed the sarcasm, professors are not the richest people. They provide a tangible proof that ideas due not make instant success.

Another common misbelief about entrepreneurship is that it means you will be rich. This is the most untrue belief on the subject. Every business venture is different. Every entrepreneur is different. There are many reasons that will lead to failure or success, but none are set in stone because you call yourself an entrepreneur. The success rate will depend on the individual efforts, market, product viability, funding, exposure, and more.

Some entrepreneurs do find financial success. Others will be drawn to the flexibility of controlling how or when you make revenues. The term rich is also subjective because someone who started in poverty will have a different experience than someone who lives off a trust fund with each having their own understanding of what is possible.

If you only seek money in your entrepreneur journey you may find success to be a fleeting goal. Some businesses make billions of dollars in revenues but do not make money. When you begin operating your own venture you will find that the money you accept for selling whatever you created will be well spoken for before you get your cut.

You are the last one who gets paid in your own business. The bills will add up as your business creates momentum meaning the more you sell the more you will spend on production. There are a lot of people who are rich on a balance sheet but lack access to real money. This is the reality of entrepreneur life that many people cannot understand or handle. Be realistic in your expectations to avoid creating a negative response to the perils of building the business. There are many more rewards than just the cash you carry in your bank account that you should consider.

One area many people think they will be rewarded in their new business is personal time. The truth is that you will be able to create your own schedule. The harder part is that you will also be responsible for holding yourself accountable for being a reliable leader in your business. You will be setting the culture by your choice to be someone who spends a lot of time working your business or the boss who everyone knows will be several hours late for work every day.

No one will make you do anything in your own business. You have an ethical responsibility however to lead your new business team by example. Your reputation will be well known in the industry by clients, vendors, and others who you deal with daily. I have stated numerous times that success is about consistency, and no other place is this true than in your punctuality, reliability, and responsibility in your duties as the leader of your company.

I believe that you must put in the work when it is time to get things done. This is best accomplished by maximizing your time by being on-time then getting directly to work. If you want personal time away from your venture then earn it through efficiency of your processes. A common personality trait of successful

35

entrepreneurs is having a high energy level to be able to outwork your team when required. You set the bar for every expectation for how your team will work therefore you must ensure you are the example you want them to be for the work ethic expected.

You will be the boss of your company. This statement is true in many aspects of business. It does not mean that you are not accountable to anyone. The business structure you create will determine who you are accountable to for your business requirements. Many entrepreneurs will run their businesses from the leadership position understanding they are ultimately accountable to their customers for ensuring the product or service is delivered as you have promised them in your advertising. If you put out substandard efforts it will show in your product. Customers will hold you accountable through refunds, credit card disputes, or poor reviews online. This will create a negative business reputation preventing you from reaching your full potential. Never mistake being the boss with being able to pass the blame because when a business fails it can always be traced back to the leader who set the example for the team to follow.

There are thousands of misbeliefs about the path you have chosen. The good thing is that you do not have to fall into the traps that other entrepreneurs get caught. You are now aware of this dilemma so you should be able to navigate around the problems that others may find themselves. The most important thing to remember is to always understand your company's core values because they will always ensure you are making decisions for the right reasons.

I challenge you to make your core values when you are launching your company to integrate them into every decision that is made from the very start. Core values are the reminders of what your company stands for to ensure your entire team has a set of common values. This is the way you mitigate subjectivity up and down your chain of command because all decisions should be made in relation to the set core values, not the individual's preference.

The core values you decide on should be the values that represent what your company stands for in all aspects of life. My personal core values include integrity first, service before self, and excellence in all I do. These are the core values that the US Air Force taught me when I was a recruit in basic training. I had arrived at basic training with no record of success in my life. I had been a very skilled baseball player, but I was lazy. This left me with little options when I barely graduated

37

from high school. I knew that I had to change to become the person I always felt I could be but had never been given the opportunity due to the common barriers most low-income children face.

The core values were a major contributing factor to my success as an entrepreneur. I use those values as my personal guide for making decisions. There are times when we all fall short of meeting our expectations we have for ourselves. The truth is that you will be your own worst critic. Core values are a tool that creates a foundation for your to compare your performance to the expectations you have set for yourself. These core values will act as your internal GPS to keep you on your path to success.

Instilling core values into your business will give you a competitive edge in your industry because they will keep your standard of performance consistent. The consistency of how people consider you in relation to your competitors will be a determining factor for your business being chosen over other similar ones. Always remember people do not buy products, they buy first into the people of the company then they buy whatever they are selling. Core values will create this consistent service level for all customers no matter who they deal with in your business the experience will be the same.

This is the secret to overcoming all the misbeliefs in the entrepreneur world. If you are a person other people want to follow, you create a solution to a problem that others are willing to pay you for, and your business model follows positive core values to create a consistency for your customer experience then you will find success as an entrepreneur. The truth about the misbeliefs of entrepreneurship is that most are created by people who either have never attempted to do it or by ill prepared people who blamed any reason they could create instead of using the core value of accountability for their own failure.

How Do I Get Started?

The choice to become an entrepreneur should always start with an idea about what product, service, or innovation that you will create. Your vision should be to solve a specific problem that will be a benefit to a significant amount of people. The new creation must have a potential customer base for the new venture to be viable. Just because you have created something cool or fun does not make it a marketable concept. You must take the time to research your market to ensure the time you will not be wasted.

I have found the best ideas come after you have immersed yourself into the study of your industry of choice. My secret to developing ideas is to continually study books on the subjects that interest me. I choose subjects I enjoy because the information you put into your mind will begin to create the thoughts that you generate. This is important to understand because many of the popular influences in today's world create extremely negative information inputs into your mind. There are extreme negative influences that people do not filter because it is considered cool to include social media, pop culture, video games, and other addictive activities that add little value to your life. These

40

influences steal your focus while providing useless influences on your thoughts.

I make a very concerted effort to control the information that I allow into my mind. I only partake in activities that provide positive influences on my thought process. I study books consistently that are on subjects in the markets that I am interested in entering. This creates the mental conditions to create new innovative concepts that I can evaluate for potential business opportunities. My process causes me to have creative awakening where I wake up in the middle of the night from lucid dreams where an entire idea is presented in my mind.

I keep an idea notebook nearby so when I awake from these dreams I can immediately start writing down everything I can remember before the idea is lost. My process is more extreme than most people because I do not listen to the radio in my vehicle or watch a lot of television because most modern entertainment is toxic to the innovative process. The rule of thumb is that every thought that you put into your mind your brain will think on it as it processes the concept. It will attempt to problem-solve the information. Therefore people who listen to certain music or follow celebrity social media will begin emulating these influences without even realizing it. I believe that if you want to change the person you are then you need to start with what you consume with your mind.

I recommend that you take a few minutes to make a list of your daily activities or even spend a week writing down everything you do. Then evaluate all the influences that you commonly are consuming. You may find yourself shocked at the amount of negativity that you are experiencing daily, but the good news is you can fix this if you desire. You can improve your influences by making better choices for the information you allow into your life and seek positive role models in the industries you are interested in exploring.

My favorite influencers are people who have achieved the levels of success that I wish to reach. Your choices should not be people on your current level or below it because they will only keep you the same as you are today. I see this common mistake being made where ambitious people seek the advice of the people closest to them but only end up having their dreams destroyed. This happened to me when I told my family I was starting my own business. Every person closest to me tore the idea apart. This is because they had not walked the path I was choosing. They feared to leave their comfort zones.

You must choose entrepreneurs to study or gain mentorship from who have already walked the path you are embarking on to learn the hard lessons they learned through trial and error. This will allow you to improve on their successes instead of attempting to relive the missteps others have already experienced. You will have your own issues that will be unique to the entrepreneurial journey that you will have to figure out. By studying other successful people you gain an advantage in your market.

When you drive a car somewhere do you take the freeway or drive through the forest that has no roads? Unless you are an avid adventurer, the answer will be to take the freeway because the path had already been cleared making the journey is faster. Successful people are an amazing source of information about the trials of being an entrepreneur. You must take time to study your craft.

I approach being an entrepreneur the same as a baseball player approaches their sport. Professional baseball players spend their time taking thousands of pitches for batting practice, thousands of ground balls for fielding practice, and watch hundreds of hours of video of their games to gain a competitive advantage. What

43

makes you better than a highly talented professional athlete? The answer is you are not. You should recognize the amount of training each top tier professional puts into their readiness training.

The average wantrepreneur assumes that they already have all the answers. They do not engage in the professional development training required to be successful. Their shortsightedness will eventually lead to failure for their business because you cannot omit the preparation required to be the best. Entrepreneurial success requires that you always be honest with yourself. You must take time to engage in only the activities that create a positive result that moves you towards your set goals.

Developing Your Business Ideas

I stated previously that I maintain an idea notebook where I keep a record of concepts that I get inspirations for throughout the day. I find myself thinking of new ideas constantly because I am fully engaged in the study of business, technology, industry, leadership, and many other subjects. My mind is always problem-solving these areas. I find that inspiration comes day and night. I am always prepared to capture these ideas in order to further explore them through my development process.

44

The first step I always take is to **identify the problem** the new idea is most closely related to be able to further explore its business viability. The easiest place to start researching the background of a problem is to do a simple Google search on the subject. The first page results will determine what people are thinking about the concept, or if they are worried about it at all. The first page of Google will normally be filled with businesses that have developed their websites towards a targeted keyword. If there are no business sites served up then this means that other businesses are not attacking the market.

This can mean that other businesses have conducted their research and did not find the concept worth exploring any further or that no one has identified your specific solution. Either result will still require further investigation to ensure you know enough about the idea to decide to proceed with its development or not. Do not be discouraged if the search results do not produce valid content because you may have identified an issue that others have yet to find.

The best method for conducting your research is to continually ask questions about the subject. Asking questions is the best way to keep your search on track

45

and formulating the questions to ask will keep your investigation on target. A common error I see people make is that they approach business issues with a "scatter-brained" approach. This is not productive because as an entrepreneur your most valuable asset is your personal time. Asking these types of questions will keep you on target;

- Is this an ongoing issue that requires a permanent solution?

- How long has the problem been occurring?

- Did my research find any usable data on the subject?

- Are other people talking about the issue?

- What was the search volume for the keywords about the issue?

- Did I find any competitors already in the market?

These questions are an example of the ones you can create to identify your potential market. The great thing about it is that there are no wrong questions to ask if the questions stay focused on your primary goal of

46

identifying whether the new idea is worth turning into a business. Just always remember to use an analytical approach to this to evaluate if you are proceeding because of good data or because you have become emotionally attached to your idea.

Researching Your Target Market

If you have identified a concept that you decide has potential through your initial research the next step is to **clarify the problem** by taking a deeper look at the analytic data that you accumulate. There are a lot of excellent sources for conducting this research, but I prefer to use Google's tools because they are free. One goal of this book is to provide you with the most cost-effective methods for creating your own entrepreneurial opportunities. These tools include many free options. I most commonly use Google Trends and Google Keyword Planner.

Google Trends is an amazing tool that allows you to see the volume of search traffic worldwide for any subject. It is very easy to use and requires you to simply enter a keyword you want information about. It will return the data. The first data you will see is the "popularity" of the search term. Google rates this on a scale from 0-100, with zero meaning there is no interest and 100 meaning the topic is very popular. My test

47

search was for the keyword "youth entrepreneurship". The results are very promising because over the past 12 months this keyword has a rating of nearly 100 consistently.

Google Trends should always be used to determine if your business ideas are valid. This is because the success of the idea is not based on your emotional attachment to it. The success of the idea will be directly related to whether people want to purchase it. It is also important to know if they are searching for something related to it. The customers will decide all successful products or services in the end. Google Trends is the best representation of this need.

Google Keyword Planner is another tool that will give you analytic data that is related to your idea. The difference from Google Trends is that it not only returns average search volume it will also breakdown the search volume by specific keywords to give a more developed look at how people are searching for the concept. This tool is part of Google's multi-billion-dollar digital advertising platform that businesses use to advertise their products or services. The best part is that it is free to use with your Google account login.

My test search for our term "youth entrepreneurship" returned 30 keywords that are consistently used to search for these types of programs. The report is easily downloadable to an excel sheet where you can easily sort your data using the program's tabs at the top of the page. The information for my test search gave me not only the keywords used but also;

- Average searches per month

- Average "cost per click" for advertising

- Competition for the keywords

- "Top of Page" bid cost (low & high)

This data is very important for your decision making both in the conceptual stage we are discussing and in the execution stage, we will discuss later. The best indication for you to proceed with your idea is the number of searches people are doing. Google Keyword Planner gives you the most in-depth look at this information. I also want to judge the level of competition for each concept. This program clearly shows you whether other businesses are pursuing your market.

Competition is a misunderstood thing in business. The wantrepreneurs consistently repeat a lot of

49

nonsensical ideas they see on their social media pages or in books about the subject. I believe that this causes confusion for new entrepreneurs because many of them take the words of people to heart then jump into markets that are saturated with competitors. I prefer to identify markets that have large search volumes but lighter competition. This will make the entry into the market easier and reduces the cost of advertising to get your new business concept in front of potential customers.

The common belief that is regurgitated online is "competition is good". If you are trying to build your empire then you should want to dominate the market or do not enter it at all. If you attempt to play it safe and set your goals to get a "piece of the market" then you are setting yourself up to meet the status quo. You are essentially seeking to be mediocre which will ensure your failure. When you decide to enter a market, always do it with the intentions of doing it ten times better than your competition. You must dominate in every aspect of what your business provides to your customer.

Once you have decided your business concept is valid due to the research from the analytic data you have accumulated then you will be ready to move on to the launch phase of this process. Only make this decision if the data supports your concept and not because you are

50

Ellis Franks "The Next Bezos: Your Path To Entrepreneurship"

in love with the idea. Entrepreneurs must curb their
emotional attachments in this critical phase. You must
save those emotions for when they will be needed when
you are selling your new venture to customers. Data
does not lie. Trust the data before moving forward and
you will be more successful when you launch your
business venture.

Launching Your Concept

Now that you have decided that your idea is
worth turning into a functioning business you are ready
to start planning for the future of your business. The
first thing I recommend is that you define the goals for
your business to create a framework for what you are
creating. The goal should be to make a profit. Your
additional goals should include the purpose for which
your business will function whether it is to sell products,
provide a service, or to create a charitable program that
helps others. These goals should meet three elements to
be effective;

- Specific

- Measurable

- Attainable

51

The business goals should be specific to ensure the purpose of the business is clearly defined. I have witnessed a lot of business owners who fail to follow this advice. They end up straying from their primary purpose only to find themselves spread too thin to be effective in any area. Entrepreneurs cannot afford to be scatterbrained in their efforts because time is a limited asset you will have. It must be effectively managed. Goals that are specific are like the "Google Maps" of your business that keeps you on track as you build your concept.

Goals should also be measurable in every facet of your new idea. You will be the leader of your business. You must create a system and culture that rewards meeting your set expectations for the quantity, quality, and timeliness of all work performed. Entrepreneurial ventures will always have limits on resources. Measuring your business goals frequently will ensure that you are not wasting these precious resources needlessly. I also believe that every business should create a system of rewards that recognizes people who consistently exceed the measurable pieces of your process because these workers, or yourself in a self-operated venture, help save on business expenses through their diligent efforts and should never be marginalized.

Measuring your goals is very important to manage your budgets and for projecting future expenses for your business. There is an abundance of tools you can use for every business function. My most commonly used, that are free, are Google Drive, Google Analytics, Google Webmaster Tools, Google Docs, Google Calendar, and a host of other complimentary services on the search engine provider. These free services are very useful for setting up project management tools within to be able to ensure your project stays on track.

If you are new to Google's functions, you may be asking yourself how do I use those? The good news is that it is very simple to create your system for tracking your goals with these tools. I prefer to use them in the following ways;

> **Google Docs**: save all business forms, contracts, marketing materials, agendas, schedules, etc.

- Give or limit access to members of your team

- Create tracking spreadsheets to monitor progress

- Makes a centralized filing area for all your important paperwork

53

<u>Google Calendar</u>: used to create your scheduling for all your important meetings.

- Set your meetings and invite employees or clients

- Create alerts for meetings or due dates for projects

- Use to for your sales teams to schedule sales calls and follow-up appointments

<u>Google Drive</u>: The location where all your data is stored

- Use this as a digital filing system

<u>Google Analytics</u>: Connect your digital assets to this tool to track traffic to your sites

- A perfect tool to decide target marketing for campaigns

- Provides demographic data for the types of people who are visiting your sites

- Can be used to custom site information to the people who are visiting based on very targeted information the program returns

- Provides data for areas that are not performing well to make decisions to either increase or abandon marketing campaigns

  Google Webmaster Tools: Provides additional marketing analytics and site performance to help you better understand how your digital media is performing

These are not the only tools available but are a sample of the options you have access to use for free. There are a host of paid services that you can purchase but I like to be as frugal as possible with my business expenses. These tools are very good for meeting the needs of a startup. If your business grows too large for these programs to support your needs you can find a host of companies that provide professional assistance in every area of business. I recommend you always look for the best "value" over the best "price" when making these decisions.

Now that your goals are measurable you must now evaluate them to ensure they are attainable. Unfortunately, the internet is full of fakers that will lead you to believe that by spending $99.99 today you can become a billionaire in forty-five days. This sets an

55

irrational expectation for potential entrepreneurs in terms of how to decide if something is attainable. Never compare your venture to anything else except your goals. If you are meeting your goals and your business is growing as expected, then you are on track. The error many young entrepreneurs make is that they attempt to seek validation for their efforts by way of social media. They attempt to "show off" or even worse fake success to impress people to gain followership. This is a trap for you and your venture because it violates the integrity of what you are building. You are not in competition with anyone. You are in competition with yourself and your ability to convince actual customers to purchase what your business is providing.

The hit television show "The Shark Tank" highlights this error young entrepreneurs make. Nearly every one of the business owners that makes false predictions about their businesses is laughed off the stage by the "Sharks" who are very seasoned investors. These entrepreneurs have simply violated the principle of ensuring their goals are attainable. The overvaluation of their business only fools them and not investors. The best way to prevent this is to use your measurable data to make conservative predictions about your future growth. You must always assume that your projections will require 10X the effort, money, and time required than you have estimated. This is how you keep your goals attainable and realistic.

The next step after creating your goals is to develop your action plan. I prefer to use a whiteboard for my entire process and especially when I create the action plan. The action plan is the guideline that you will use to understand where you are at in relation to your goals. The action plan is most closely like the game plan a coach creates each week for their teams that outlines the actions the team will take in every situation during their upcoming game.

Your action plan should identify the course of actions your business needs to take to keep on track to include identifying every task that needs to be completed, who is assigned to each task, and the due dates for each action that must be completed. The tasks should be measured by three things;

- **Quantity**: how much work is expected to be completed

- **Quality**: the acceptable level of performance the task is expected to be completed

- **Timeliness**: minimum time allotted to complete the task

Entrepreneurs should evaluate every performance based on the quality, quantity, and timeliness of the work that is performed. This includes the individual performance of the team members and the tasks they are working to complete. This is the fairest method of judging your business performance by ensuring your venture launch is staying on track.

The last part of this process is to be actively engaged in your processes. You must remain open-minded to the feedback your analytic data provides you as you execute your action plan. The execution stage is all about receiving feedback and adjusting the real-world information your system is providing you. There is no place for emotions in this process. I warn you like the new entrepreneur that becoming emotionally attached to any portion of your plan can lead to failure for the entire business. Trust the data and adjust your plan to meet your customer's needs. Data is your guide, not your ego.

The process for executing your action plan is simple. You should have identified all the tasks required and set timelines for their completion by this point. You should always also have your analytic data for reference to give you real-time information about your venture.

Now you must simply evaluate – adjust – repeat with your process.

Create Your Business Structure

Your entrepreneurial venture will also require some important legal tasks to be completed. If you are under 18 years old, you may have to get your parents to either complete these tasks or make them an official partner with rights to complete legal business registration. This is not a complex task. A Google search will return a lot of articles on what you are required for your city and state to register the type of business you are creating. Beware of the businesses that prey on unsuspecting business owners in this phase of their process because they charge large sums of money for completing tasks you can easily do yourself.

This part of your process will require you to choose an official business name, register the business name with your state, file for a federal tax identification, and choose the most appropriate method for your business to receive payments. It is not the glamorous part of entrepreneurship, but it is legally mandatory and must be completed. The best part is that it is very simple and not very expensive to complete.

60

Choosing A Business Name

The first thing to do is to decide what you will name your company. This is an exciting part of the process because it is the beginning of something that maybe the next Apple or Google and choosing the right name is important. The name of your business should be something that speaks to your audience and allows for your purpose to be easily identifiable. Do not worry if you choose wrong to start, you can rename your company later, but if you spend years building a reputation for a brand you will essentially be starting over at that point.

The best method for choosing a business name is to brainstorm by writing down every thought that comes to your mind about your company. Make a list of anything you believe is relatable and then sit down with your team or alone to sift through the ideas you created. Use the brainstorming list to create your top ten list of names then search the internet using them to see what search results you get back.

This is important to not cause a confusing situation where your business has the same name as another company or even worse it will let you know of the types of content that are served up when your potential customers search for that name. There is no worse of an error than a cool name chosen that leads your customers to inappropriate content online so make sure whatever name you choose has passed this test before you register your business name.

Once you have decided on what you will call your business you are ready to officially register the business with your state's business registry department. The rules for business registration are state-specific. I recommend you Google the steps required before you start to understand the process required for your state.

Legal Registration

Legally registering your business will require you to visit the online site for the state agency that deals with businesses. This is usually the state government's website. I found with several test searches for various states that it is easy to find yours by searching Google: "register business <STATE>" and the searches will return the site address. Watch out for companies who are selling services. They will be identifiable because they appear at the top of the page with the word "ad" somewhere around their information. This is usually found just under the ad heading on the second line on Google.

You will be required to choose the type of business you will create. The new venture will either be created as a "sole proprietorship" or "limited liability corporation" (LLC). I recommend that you choose the LLC because it provides some protections for you as an individual. The choice is ultimately yours. If you are lucky to have a financial advisor who is astute at business law then they may recommend another entity structure that better suits your needs. If you have any questions about the types of business structures I recommend doing a Google search. Read about all the various options available to better make your decision.

How To Get A Federal Tax ID

The process to obtain your Federal Tax Identification for your business is the easiest step in your process. Once you have legally registered your business name you will need to go to the below link to follow the steps on the site. This is a free registration. If you are prompted to pay then you are not on the IRS website and need to leave immediately.

https://www.irs.gov/businesses/small-businesses-self-employed/apply-for-an-employer-identification-number-ein-online

How Does My Business Get Paid?

Now we have arrived at the step in your business set-up that is the most exciting, how you receive payments from your customers. If you have successfully registered your business and acquired a Federal Tax Identification, then you can now open a business banking account and sign up for a credit card service. The previous steps must be completed before moving on to this step or you will not be allowed to open either account.

The choice of bank is a personal preference and some banks cater to businesses while others are not as business friendly. You can choose any bank you prefer to set up your business account. Most will attempt to sell you their partnered credit card processing services. These additional services are sold to you for a commission from the bank employee. The services will work fine but require extensive paperwork in most cases.

I recommend using a service such as Clover or Square because they are designed to be simple and mobile. Most businesses today require mobility. Traditional credit card processing services tend to be

64

severely outdated and not user-friendly. Square is the service that I use. It is acceptable for the needs of my businesses.

Square allows you to be able to create invoices both on your mobile devices and computer interface. I like the flexibility of the service and the companion mobile apps make conducting business very easy. I can complete my entire sales process from the sales meeting to invoicing to charging the customers card onsite when I close deals for my various businesses. I can also generate real-time reporting for my sales anywhere in the world ensuring I am always on track with meeting my daily sales goals.

My only complaint with the mobile app-based services is that they provide only minimum fraud protections for businesses. Every business will face fraud from unscrupulous customers. I have found that traditional credit card processing services provide much better fraud support for entrepreneurs than mobile apps. You must determine which service works best for your business by weighing the pros and cons of each versus the types of transactions your business deals with regularly.

Once you have chosen the system that works best for you then your business is ready to make money.

Marketing Your Venture

The most fun you will have after collecting payments is marketing your business. I have previously warned you against becoming emotional when making business decisions. Now is the time to release all the pent-up excitement that you have contained within you. Marketing your business is where your passion belongs. You can release this passion at will. People do not buy products or services, they buy into the people behind these things.

Doubt this reasoning? Then look at the line at an Apple retail store the day, or even sometimes a week, of a big release of a hot new product. Apple users do not buy these products because they are the best, they bought into the vision that the late CEO Steve Jobs created as the culture for his company and brand. You must market your business with the same passion that Jobs displayed. Create an experience for your customers that is unlike anything they can experience anywhere else.

The most successful entrepreneurs are the ones that live for their business. They champion their vision everywhere they go. I have found that customers come to you in the strangest places. I have closed deals

67

anywhere you can imagine from shopping lines to gas station parking lots to friend's houses and more. When you live your dream and show a passion for it you will attract people to whatever you are creating.

I have found that entrepreneurs who start with large sums of money will lack the passion required and refuse to do the things necessary to make their businesses a success. Sometimes money can make the entrepreneur lazy or entitled. This causes their businesses suffer. The history of Silicon Valley is littered with failed companies who thought the billions of dollars invested in them would make them a success, but they failed. Their fatal error was thinking that money would work for their venture and make it successful. Money indeed makes things a lot easier, but it will not guarantee success.

Passionate entrepreneurs are the best advertising for their business. They make the most lasting impression with their potential customers. People want to be part of something bigger than themselves. This why social media is so popular. If you can live for your venture and sell your passion for it everywhere you go, then people will want to buy from you no matter what you are selling.

68

Your goal will be to bottle that passion into every advertising method available to create a dominate marketing program that makes your business successful. The methods I teach people to use include creating websites that speak to your customers, building engaging social media that activates your following, creating a culture within your business that gets your business in front of as many people as possible, and being able to sale your business ideas to people when opportunity finds you in those awkward moments that you think you are off-duty. An entrepreneur is never off-duty if they want to be successful.

Your goal is to be visible everywhere people are looking for your product, service, or related purchases they are considering. Most purchases start with the potential buyer visiting the internet to do their research. Most businesses will have a website which means you will have competition for the "online real estate" on page one of Google. I will teach you how to create a marketing behemoth that will make profits and dominate your market.

How To Make A Website

If I asked you to decide whether a Lamborghini or a Prius would win in a test of max speed you could easily pick the winner of this test. The same cannot be said for websites that represent businesses that pop up on Google or Facebook that should be designed just like that Lamborghini but most function like an out of gas Prius. I know most people are thinking, a website is a website, but this is very far from the truth. I ran a major national business for a short time that had no products but made millions of dollars selling other people's products or services. We were able to dominate the markets because we built 10,000s of websites for locations nationwide that captured all the local businesses traffic. Then we funneled those customers to the business owners after we made a substantial profit. Most times we made as much as the local owner made because we were able to dictate the prices by controlling the internet.

Essentially, we were the Lamborghini racing against the Prius. Many times racing against no other opponent at all. Creating this type of website is your next project. It is the most exciting part of the entire business cycle for me. I will break down the steps required for you to turn your website into a dominant force in your market by identifying the process for

70

ensuring your website ranks as high in search engines as possible.

The choice for selecting the home for your website is based on your ability to code. If you are a seasoned coder the options for creating a site are vast and the flexibility to create any type of functionality is high. I will for the purpose of this book give the novice website builder advice on choosing a user-friendly option for creating a site that can be easily managed and perform at a high level.

If you perform a search on Google for website builders, you will find a variety of options available to use. My search returned results for Wix, Weebly, Squarespace, Google, GoDaddy, and several others that most people have heard of because of their advertising. Each one of these sites will work for the novice site builder and each offers varying levels of support and services once you are their customer.

I recommend that if you are new to site building you choose one that has the easiest user interface and the one that has the best "drag & drop" functionality. This means that the site coders have already coded all the different tools you will need to build your site. You can

71

drag the parts from the tool menu to the page and create your site with ease. The two most popular for this type of website building are Wix.com and Weebly.com. Either site will allow you to create an excellent website.

The process for creating your website can vary as there is no true creative process for creating it. I like to sit down to sketch out an overview of the pages and content I will end up creating before starting the building process. This is not mandatory. I prefer an idea of what I want to create before starting a project that I am very familiar with in terms of content.

If I am not familiar with the content for a website I am building I will start with researching the market. I look at competitors to see what is already created. This allows me to familiarize myself with the consistent content others have created. I take note of colors used, layouts, pictures, and the content the copywriters created to see what they believe the customers are looking for when they are shopping. Once I have enough inspiration, I will begin my process of creating the framework for the site.

I always start with creating the main pages that the site will show on the homepage. The most common

72

pages include the homepage, about us page, contact
page, picture gallery, and product or service pages.
These pages are my starting framework for the site. I
use them just like a construction foreman uses the
concrete foundation that is poured prior to building any
other part of the house. These pages may change as the
website is developed and the final design is realized.
They layout how my site will flow. The initial layout is
not as important because in the final stages of the site
build things will get reorganized a lot of times because
as the site comes together the identity will become more
evident.

The most important part of your website is the
content you create. This means the copywriting, the
story you tell with the words, on the site is the most
valuable area that should be considered when creating
the site. The content will connect your passion to your
customer's needs. It will represent what your business
stands for online. The content you create should be
natural and direct, speaking to your customer as if they
are standing in front of you. The content should also
address the questions the customer has about your
services. I recommend that you brainstorm anything the
customer may ask before starting to write out your
website's copy to ensure you address these questions.
You should also take all the feedback customers to give
you to update your content to ensure the real-time needs

73

of the customer is being met by your site. Customers will be the best source of improvements for your website. You should actively engage them in their experiences on the site.

Once you have created natural content that speaks to your customer then you must take steps to ensure that the search engines will find your content. These search engines use algorithms that rate your pages' content for validity. They rate website content against the chosen search keywords the customer is looking for when they enter their search box. This process happens in milliseconds. The search engine's algorithm decides the top ten pages that meet the search each customer is entering out of the billions of pages within the Google server. Getting your website served up to the top of Google searches is a highly coveted. It is a multi-billion-dollar industry that I will teach you how to compete with easily in any market.

How Can People Find Me On Google?

The truth is that the Google secret formula is a highly protected asset the search engine giant protects better than the gold in Fort Knox. The internet is full of posers who claim they are "Search Engine Marketing Experts". For a large price, they will guarantee that your site will be ranked at the top of Google. This is a

74

fraudulent statement because only the Google algorithm will decide if this happens. It makes this decision individually with each search that a person enters.

The way the system works is the person searching online enters a keyword into the search bar. Keywords are the chain of words that represent what you are looking to find. The search engine algorithm then works its magic by evaluating the words individually and together before comparing the content of hundreds of millions of pages in the Google Index. The algorithm returns the top related results nearly instantly. It ranks each page served up based on its weighted content. If you search again the results may shuffle because each time you do the same search the algorithm repeats its process fully no matter how many times you repeat the search.

The reason is that the algorithm is evaluating the search on many weighted factors that is kept a secret. This includes the personal data each Google user has stored in their histories to produce a personalized search result. Google recommends that you create your website with good content about the information you want to provide to searchers. Once created you must register your site with their Webmaster Tools to be able to submit your pages directly to the Google indexing

75

database. This is not mandatory to have a site, but it is the fastest way to get your content into the Google Index.

This may sound confusing, but it is simple. It means you must create good content and submit it to Google. After that the search engine will do the rest. This is only half of the needed things that you should do to ensure you are being evaluated to the best of your abilities by the Google algorithm.

Other things that you need to ensure is that your content is created with copywriting that effectively uses the keywords you want to target. I have been contracted to fix a lot of business websites. This has included major companies that many people recognize but were not showing up for search results. The most common reason I found was because they failed to create good content. The content they had did not have a single keyword for the products or services they were selling. This would be like showing up for school but forgetting your books, lunch, and clothes because though you may be present you will not be able to function. Even worse, you will more than likely be kicked out for not meeting the standards required.

Google evaluates all the words on your site, which is your content. It then ranks it compared to the other few hundred million sites for "relevancy". When a search is entered the algorithm ranks every site from one to thousands of pages deep. The top-ranked sites will be displayed on the coveted page one of Google. These pages that are on this main search page result will end up receiving over 85 percent of all the business for that keyword because studies have shown that most searchers never look past page one. This makes your need to properly format your copywriting on your website critical to your business's success.

The secret, this is the part that you must listen to closely if you listen to no other part, is to ensure your website elements all contain the keywords that you desire to be found by your customers;

- Page Name

- Page Title

- Page URL

- Page Description

- Copywriting

- Content Headers

- Content Body

Most of these items are found in your website's tool menu under "advanced settings" or "SEO settings". It is a fatal mistake to overlook this requirement because no matter how amazing your website looks without these minimum items being met your site will never be found.

This is the dilemma that the national deli franchise called "Schlotzsky's" faces with their website. The site is a national website that lacks good content. The pages are not optimized in accordance with Google's minimum standards causing it to be ranked very low in search results. The common attempt this company's web development team has made to target the geo-specific search targeting that Google has recently deployed was to make location pages with the addresses of all their locations, but no content other than that.

If a company like Schlotzsky's properly optimized their entire site with very good, keyword-rich content then they would dominate every search result because of the size of their brand and the expanse of their reach. Instead, the company does not even seem to notice that their website gets pushed out of page one results many times by more aggressive locals deli

78

websites that have taken the proper steps to optimize their sites.

You will be better prepared to dominate your market because you will understand how to get your pages found in Google and other search engines. This knowledge will save you a lot of money that you would otherwise spend on "pay-per-click" (PPC) ads. The difference in organically optimizing your website and relying on paid ads is that your optimized site will show up 24 hours a day for every search term you optimize it for, but the PPC ads only show up if your budgets remain.

Studies also show that organic pages receive around 85 percent of all page clicks. This means that PPC ads account for only 15 percent of page clicks, but companies spend around 90 percent of their advertising budgets on PPC ads. This is a competitive advantage for the industrious entrepreneur that takes the time to properly develop their websites with content that the search engines rank as extremely relevant to ensure you are served up on the first search page.

Additionally, you must register your business and website with Google. You can create a free business listing on "Google My Business" that will be verified by the search engine. Once your verification is approved Google will serve up your business listing to potential customers based on their keyword searches.

You must also request a verification card be sent to your business address from Google. The card will arrive within two weeks of your request. It will contain a serial number that you enter your business listing account for verification. The best thing about verification is that once verified your business will be added to all of Google's search tabs such as Google Maps and Google Reviews.

Should List My Business On Other Sites?

The answer to this question is YES! You should have a business profile on any site that will allow you to register. Top tier sites such as Yelp, Home Advisor, Angie's List, and other sites like them provide excellent backlinks to your site. Google likes these and your site value will increase with every site you register your business information with a strong website link.

Social media sites will also be a very strong backlink source for your site. Creating business pages on social media increases your business's exposure

80

online. The added value is that these sites also provide strong links that add to your site's rank in the Google ranking system.

Create Your Social Media

Today social media is intertwined into every part of our lives. Your business can take advantage of the engaged users of these platforms by creating engaging content. The best entrepreneurs will create advocate customers who tell everyone they know about the exceptional experiences they had with your brand.

The goal is to create these social media pages as a place where you and your customers can interact. The fatal error I see with a lot of businesses is that they never utilize their pages causing a loss of value of for the social media. The best accounts document everything. They tell their stories through the content created on their social media. The more these businesses engage their followers results in more success for their brands.

There are a lot of social media sites to manage. We will discuss not just the sites that are the most popular, but also cool management tools you can use to present your content. This lesson will ensure you not only is your business connected, but it will also stay

81

actively engaged with professional techniques to make your job easier. Before we get ahead of ourselves let's look at a few popular and must-have social media sites for you to explore.

Facebook

Facebook is home to over 2.38 billion monthly users as of 2019. Many users live on the site and are always looking for new and exciting content to share with their friends. The social media giant allows businesses to create professional pages to represent your brands and engage with users looking for the things you are selling.

It is very easy to create your business page. The site also has an abundance of tools for businesses to enhance their followers' experience. Some professionals specialize in designing professional pages for businesses at a cost. The best function Facebook offers is its advertising platform that is very easy to use.

Facebook advertising is an affordable way to gain followership or promote your business. The system algorithm allows you to get your ads directly in front of the people you are targeting. The in-depth data that the site stores on every user is used to create customer profiles that the advertising system uses to its advantage. There is no pay-per-click system that knows more about their customers than Facebook. The best part is that it is simple to use.

Facebook is an excellent branding tool for any business. I also believe it is a very good method of connecting with your customers due to the tools each business page offers. The social site allows you to connect with customers direct to your mobile phone through the messaging system. It also has an accountability tracker to let you see how well you handle customer contacts based on response times. This is very important because customers who are left with unanswered customer service issues will become frustrated. You can use these tools to give them a direct contact to you anywhere you may be which will enhance your customer service.

Instagram

Instagram is home to over 1 billion users as of 2019. Most of these users are under the age of 35 years. This makes the site a super hip place to create your business content. The site allows entrepreneurs to share their stories by sharing pictures and videos. The users engage your shared media by liking, sharing, or commenting on the media that you post.

83

There is no better way to tell your potential customers what your mission is for your business. Studies show that people engage pictures and videos at a higher rate than words. This is the lifeblood of Instagram. The set-up and use of a business account are very easy making this a perfect marketing tool for any entrepreneur.

There are a ton of media editing applications that were created just for Instagram that will make your content creating tasks easier. A quick Google search net 182 million results for the search "Instagram media editing". The top result gave an abundance of options that offered varying types of editing capabilities. The list of top Instagram editing applications included Afterlight 2, Snapspeed, Aviary, Vintagio, Tiltshift, and a dozen other options. Take a little time to find the perfect application that meets your needs and preference then get to work documenting your business activities daily as often as possible.

The best use of this platform I experienced was from a local storefront owner in San Antonio, Texas. I got to know him while I was creating his digital advertising strategy, website, site optimization, and the search engine optimization for his website. He used

84

Instagram, also Facebook Live, to host live videos of his events where he engaged the audience throughout. He would host online competitions to win free merchandise netting him thousands of dollars each week just from the videos alone. The revenues generated in the contests paid for any merchandise he gave away many times over while keeping his audience engaged. People would constantly be contacting him ready for the next event. This is the power of social media when employed in positive ways for your business.

Twitter

Twitter hosts over 330 million users that interact through a message system that only allows 140 characters per post. The site is an experience in brevity where you must condense your messages into short posts that can have accompanying media if you desire. The site is the most active with the use of hashtags and these allow the entrepreneur to create links to communities on the site that are clickable by users.

The art of the hashtag is a skill that must be learned for any new entrepreneur who wants their content to be found. When you place a hashtag in your post users can click on them to follow a link to a thread of similar content that used the same hashtag. For example, if you were a dog groomer, you can

85

#doggroomer or #washmydog or anything like that to connect to the community. The easiest way to find out what is popular is to watch the "trending" menu on the page that will tell you what users are talking about most at that time.

I encourage you to experiment with hash tagging to push your way into the conversations that are occurring online. People are posting tweets with the hashtags to be able to track the conversation. This is a target-rich environment for you to take advantage of with your content creation. There is no better way to get your messages in front of customers than effective tagging. There are many third-party businesses that have been created that can be used to get more in-depth with the understanding of the trends occurring on Twitter that I recommend you research, test, and employ to maximize the effectiveness of your tagging strategy. If used properly you can grow your brand for free using this system by interjecting your content into trending conversations that are related. The goal with social media is to gain exposure which Twitter makes this easy.

YouTube

YouTube boasts over 1.9 billion monthly users. What is even more impressive is that these users are spending 250 million hours a day watching videos on the

86

site. That stat is proof that every entrepreneur should be engaging with potential customers on the platform.

The site requires a little more work to create your content but the value for return on the investment is high. The site is also a huge platform for advertising and this option should be exploited. You can create banner ads or video ads to promote your business to reach highly engaged users on the network.

Another method used to maximize the popularity of YouTube is to create "how-to videos" for your industry. You are the subject matter expert on the business you have created. You have knowledge that people are searching for if you have created a solution to a problem that is universally required by others. These videos can be the link that connects your new product with the customers who may not know a solution exists. The videos will build consumer confidence in your brand if created properly leading to potential revenues by customers.

YouTube has a very solid platform for creating videos in its video studio that is available to all YouTube subscribers. The studio allows you to edit your videos, tag them for search optimization in the site, and it allows you to manage customers interactions by giving you a platform to respond to video comments.

I recommend starting off doing free content that you create and is found organically by potential customers. After you have established your business you can move into paid advertising where you can pay to have your content promoted to users who are searching for related content. The costs are reasonable for advertising overall making this option a very good method of informing customers about your brand.

YouTube also offers an opportunity to monetize your content as you build your follower base. If your videos are popular then you can gain additional income from allowing advertisers to market their products on your content. Also as you stack up followership numbers to reach "influencer" status YouTube advertisers can solicit you to directly promote their products resulting in potential endorsement dollars. This is an avenue of revenues that will take a lot of work and very few people on the site make it to the level that the YouTube stars reach where they make millions of dollars annually. This should not be your primary goal because it is a lot like winning the lottery, it happens but to a small percent of the people chasing the dream. Be realistic in your expectations and work the content

88

creation intelligently to ensure you gain the most value from your efforts.

Social Media Management Tools

The above social media platforms are important to your success. Each will require massive actions in each area to create amazing content. Do not worry, there are social media tools available to help you manage your social presence because I understand time is your most precious resource. The best tools will allow you to manage all your social media pages from a single location, give you mobile content creation options, and allow scheduling of content release over a selected period.

There are a variety of social media management tools to choose from. Finding one is as simple as Googling "social media management tools" and you will get a ton of options. I recommend you check out the blogs on the results page that discuss the top options for social media management to make the best decision for your business.

I use Hootsuite to manage all my posts online. I have used the site for many years. I am comfortable with the functionality of the site and it allows me to

89

schedule content for months in advance. The site is very useful for entrepreneurs because you can allot time in your schedule to create content and then schedule it for delivery later. This frees you from having to post all your content one at a time. It allows you to schedule advertising posts at the intervals you prefer.

There is no wrong choice of social media management tools if you are comfortable with the platform. The goal of using a site like Hootsuite is to make your job simpler. It allows you to be present online at times when you might otherwise be unavailable. The sites do not take the place of customer engagement and should be used to enhance your social media experience.

Get Out & Tell People Your Story

I drove home a point earlier in this book that you should not become emotional in your decision-making while creating your entrepreneurial venture, but now I am going tell you to go for it. Marketing your business is the place where the emotion belongs. Your passion for your business should always be seen by your customers. The most effective way to present your company is by showing others how much love you have for your business when you are out in the community.

90

Humility is an important character trait but when you are marketing your business you will need to relax on it to let the passion out. Humility will make you want to be conservative with your advertising, but you must go all-in in this part of your venture. You should spread your story everywhere you go and always be ready with your elevator pitch. That is the condensed sales pitch you practice to be able to grab a potential client's attention in a very short amount of time. The best elevator pitch will last no longer than 30 seconds and will tell your story with passion. Do not leave home without it because the best deals I have ever made have not been in boardrooms. The nest deals I made were in times that were the least convenient but when you're ready this won't matter.

Guerilla Marketing

Guerilla marketing is the best strategy that a new entrepreneur can do because it is cost-effective. The technique is any unconventional marketing tactic that you can deploy to get your brand in front of as many customers possible and for the lowest cost. I enjoy the creative spirit behind guerilla marketing. I find that if done correctly it can be very fun.

This was my main strategy when I launched my video game truck business. Our entry to market costs was very high and made us rely on creativity with our marketing budget. I would wake up at 6 am to handwrite mailers to target customers beforehand stamping them and mailing them all. I would create about 1000 handwritten sales ads a day and worked on this every spare second I had. We also created our yard signs that later at night we would post these all over the city for the morning traffic to see. If we were lucky we might even get a few days with these ads posted before someone knocked them down.

I would also make handwritten ads that I would post on the posts of neighborhood mailboxes. You must be careful when doing this because some communities have strict laws against it so make sure you research this before trying. If you are in a city that does not have a specific law against doing it then you can use this to get your information into consumer's hands. Pay close attention to how you post anything to ensure you do not damage someone's property. Also never put anything into a mailbox because this is illegal.

Promotional Events

Promotional events can be a value to a new entrepreneur who is trying to gain exposure to the public.

92

These events are normally ones that you do for free to get in front of a lot of people. I would recommend that you use this marketing method sparingly to ensure you're not wasting time that could be spent on productive, moneymaking activities.

You will find yourself being solicited to do these types of events frequently if you own a business. My rule of thumb is that I will never give away free time for any free event when I could potentially sell my time for a profit. If I do an event like this I will find a hard to sell time in my schedule and only do the event then. You must remember that you are in business to make a profit and not to be a nonprofit to enhance someone else's profitable event.

In the end, there are no set rules for what you can do to market your business. The goal is to be passionate and tell your story to as many people as will listen. If you have a viable product or service, add the passion inside you to it, then your marketing will create a sales funnel that will propel your business to profitability.

93

Selling Is About Passion

Selling is an artform that you can learn to perfect if you are motivated. Everyone wants the glitz and glamour of being wealthy, but many times do not understand how to get it. The only way to get the things in life that you want is to be an expert at selling your business to others. Many entrepreneurs fear sales because it gets them out of their comfort zones. However, every successful business was created when someone created a vision and then was able to sell it to others to gain the "exit velocity" needed to get the venture off the ground.

Sales should not be scary. When you have created your business you should be passionate about what you are doing. This passion is the foundation to the "Law of Attraction" because that energy will attract other people to your journey if you are able to overcome your fears to sell your vision. Fear is not real anyway and knowing this is your competitive edge.

When I launched my first business I was required to come up with nearly a half million dollars to purchase the equipment needed. I had a meager savings at this point, rented my home, and did odd jobs to bring in extra money. I was in a position most people would never consider starting a business. They would not consider it

94

because the timing was not perfect. Also I did not have millionaire investors backing me.

The truth is that I did not need the perfect timing or truckloads of cash. These things would have been amazing to have on reserve to relieve the burden of launching a new business but were not necessary. I negotiated deals that covered the startup capital needed then got to work. I was able to sell others on my vision to create a paradigm where I showed them how I would be successful no matter what. Once I had the equipment I knew that I could immediately make money. I made my plans to execute my sales program to raise the capital needed as we grew the business.

I started with no money or assets but would go on to earn over a million dollars only through my efforts. I could not have done this had I not been able to sell myself to the equipment sellers and the customers that paid me for the services I sold. Everyone is a salesperson in their daily lives without realizing it. This is obvious with a little self-evaluation you will realize that everything you do in your daily life equates to you selling yourself.

When you try out for teams you are selling. When you convince your friends to see a movie you want but they do not, you are selling. When you get your parents to buy that one gift you cannot live without, you are selling. Selling is part of who you are, but it requires practice to reach a level that earns you the life you deserve.

Think of yourself as a Jedi and selling is the force. No Jedi was born being a Master and require a lifetime of training to learn to use the force in every aspect of the mystical power's abilities before being considered a master. Just like your fictitious Jedi example, you must dedicate yourself to becoming a master of selling by consistently practicing your craft.

Every entrepreneur must commit to being a student of the craft no matter if they were born with an innate talent for selling or not. You will discover that as you climb the levels of success there will be more levels to overcome. Most people set low goals like making $20 per hour, $100,000 per year, or $1 million in savings then assume when they reach these levels that they have finished. This viewpoint is shortsighted because they have not achieved those levels yet. Therefore they do not understand the dynamics of how success works when you are an entrepreneur.

96

If you possess the entrepreneurial spirit to its fullest you will find that when you surpass those "poor-mindset" milestones that opportunities will become abundant. When you first break the six-figure salary barrier you will find that now making $1 million looks tangible. When you make your first million dollars you will then see that other levels of success follow it. A true entrepreneur is a builder and collector of successes. Each successful person starts with small victories followed by major successes that grow exponentially. The higher you climb the ladder of success the more you will find yourself selling and succeeding.

Sales is about passion because it fuels the life-changing rewards that changes your entire family's path. If you are poor being a salesperson is a path to a new life. Selling does not require an MBA or prestigious college degree but is the highest paying career that anyone can join. If changing the lives of the people you love does not motivate you to become a student of sales, then this book really is not for you and you should put it down now before you waste your precious time. However, if you are getting excited about selling your business then continue to read. I will break down a few important concepts to help you build your sales understanding to prepare you for your journey.

Never Sell On Price

The most common error I see new entrepreneurs make is they believe that customers only care about the price of what they are selling. Customers are acutely aware of the costs associated with their purchases and many are very dedicated to being thrifty. The truth is that price is not a fair representation of value.

For example, if you were purchasing a car but you were only given the prices of two options available you would not be able make a valid purchase decision due to a lack of enough data on each. If the prices were $10,000 for one car and $35,000 for another if your only sales objection is the price then you would choose the cheaper one. If you made this decision solely on price you might end up with vehicle that is inoperable due to mechanical issues, damage, or some other unknown issue. The commonsense thing to do is to evaluate the overall value of each.

Therefore you must be able to sell your business based on value not price. Your job is to educate your customers to fully understand what you are selling. The important factors include the features and benefits of the product or service. You must also show that passion you

98

have for your business because people buy into the salesperson before they spend the money.

Price selling also devalues what you are selling. If you have a set price but always allow the customer to talk you into discounts then you are handing all your profits away with every devalued sale. I know this from experience in my first year as an entrepreneur. I allowed the customers to steal my services from me through discounts. The customers would call on the phone demanding I cut the price, or they would use my competitors. Out of fear I would let them set the price. The result was that at the end of that year I had lost over $85,000 in discounts. I could not afford my own utilities for over a year causing me to live without several necessities as I recovered. The customers that were beating me up of the price could afford to pay the small additional cost but wanted to see if they could take advantage of a small business because they felt entitled. Meanwhile, we were covering these losses out of pocket and deploying our equipment to mansions that were 25,000 square foot or bigger. These were the people who haggled over $100 discount.

I took this common issue to another level when my sales team was complaining about not being allowed to give discounts to close deals. I randomly chose ten customers who we provided full services then we never asked them for payment. I wanted to test the integrity of these ten randomly selected customers to show the sales team that price is irrelevant. The result was that 100 percent of the "Free Services Test Cases" never asked about paying us. They were aware they had not paid, and when we completed our services these people were all "not available" to speak to us. My sales team was astonished at this result because they had argued the customers would show integrity and offer to pay. However, not only did they accept the free services, they refused to give the customary gratuity to our service providers who went to their homes, and then we never heard from them again.

The lesson was driven home that customers will steal from you if you allow them. This is not because they are dishonest. It is because everyone feels like they deserve more. If given the opportunity to get something for free or discounted this entitlement mentality always wins over. Selling on price reinforces this mentality and should be avoided at all costs or you will squander profits then fail due to insolvency.

The proper method for selling yourself is to fully understand the problem you solve with the product or service you deliver. You must understand the core values of your business to sell the customer on them because customers want to do business with people they like and can trust. My businesses use the core values of – *integrity first, service before self, and excellence in all we do.*

These core values are integrated into every part of the services we provide. We use our value system to sell our services to validate the price we are charging. I built our sales pitches around telling our story and building value in our brand. My competitors do not understand the value of operating under core values. They fail to provide adequate services resulting in consistent no-shows for appointments, lateness, unprofessional appearance, and earn themselves very bad reviews. We value our reputation because we have tied them to our core values earning our business a reputation as the #1 service provider in our market. The side effects of this is that we have waiting lists for our service. We sell out all our appointments weekly, even at a much higher rate than other companies.

If you want to be broke and close your doors before five years then by all means sell on price only. If you want to be successful and build an empire then you must learn how to create value for your customers. Once

101

value is created then you will experience the successes
you deserve.

Creating Your Sales Pitch

Now that you understand how important selling
on value is to the success of your business you can create
your sales pitch. The pitch should tell your story while
answering all the questions that a customer may have
about what you are selling. The best sales pitches will
take the customer on a journey where your words will
create the images of them using the products that you are
selling. They should feel the emotion of how it makes
them feel. They should overcome their fear of the
unknown through your words. You should connect with
the customer throughout your pitch to create the trust
required to close the deal.

A good sales pitch will not have to mention the
price because the purchase is not about how much it
costs, the purchase is truly about how the customer can
see themselves after they have completed the deal. I use
a technique I learned for public speaking where I attach
pieces of my sales pitch to the images of customers
engaging with the services we provide. I follow a
chronological order of the customer being introduced to
our team, then showing off our equipment explaining
how our service creates a stress-free feeling throughout

102

and moves seamlessly through every detail of the services provided. I move directly into closing the deal without mentioning the price by trial-closing them by setting an appointment date. This is also called "assuming the close".

Most customers will give me all their contact information before asking me "how much" because my sales pitch sets them at ease while creating an emotional attachment to whatever I am selling. If the customer stops me to ask the price I will handle this objection by stating the price confidently. Presenting pricing information requires certainty from the salesperson. You must never attach your personal finances to the sale because the customer will recognize the emotions you present.

A common deficiency with new or weak salespeople is that they allow their own personal finances to become a bias that they portray to their own customers. The customers desire certainty from the salespeople. When someone who has not achieved a level of success financially they cannot see themselves purchasing what they are selling, and it will affect the deal. This is another place your passion for what you are selling should always shine through. If you believe in what you sell then the customer will believe in you. If

103

your customers believe in you then you will close more deals. When you close more deals you will increase your financial earnings and the cycle of success will be repeated until you achieve your goals.

Your goal is to create a sales pitch that encompasses all those features to ensure you sell your product with confidence. If your pitch is created properly then customers will spend money with you. The sales pitch is a tool that will get you to your business goals. It will also require practice to make it become second nature. You are a professional at this stage. As a professional you must engage in professional development through the study of your craft to be the best you can be.

Perfecting Your Craft

Entrepreneurs must approach their craft with the same tenacity that a professional athlete employ. The professional sports world is host to a handful of the best athletes in each sport. The competition is high though the total prospects for each sport is low. The business world is as competitive but there are tens of millions of people looking to take your place in every industry in the market. The lesson is that like professional athletes you will be required to train harder than your competition to be competitive for the long term in your market.

104

I am sure you are wondering how you can train like a professional athlete when you are selling maid services? This is a valid question. The training that you will be required to stay engaged with is the study of your market and sales techniques. The best entrepreneurs are learners first. They study their craft constantly. The average millionaire has been found to be avid learners consuming up to 53 books per year on average and should be used as a role model for you.

If you want to be a millionaire business mogul you will not find it posting selfies on social media no matter what your favorite YouTuber tells you. The path to meeting your goals is first found in the books and mentors that you learn from constantly over time. Preparing for success is important to make it lasting.

The NFL is an example of an organization that does a poor job following this principle. The league is full of millionaires who make ridiculous sums of money over their careers. The sad fact is that nearly all the players who stop playing after making millions of dollars are broke within the first two years after quitting. The fatal error of the organization is that they do not spend enough time ensuring the players are partaking in professional development in relations to their financial futures. Yes they have league rules and rookies training, but the culture is all about burning through cash as fast as they players can get it. The results are alarming as player after player becomes bankrupt each year. These players are the most gifted athletes in our country. They train hard to exceed human capabilities. Then they fail at the most important aspect of their lives because they fail to train in their craft as millionaires. The lesson is also that money does not equal success. Professional development is the path to true accomplishment in the business world.

This means that if you really want to be an entrepreneur then you must study consistently for all areas of your business. You can find mentors in the business world that speak to you because they have walked a similar path. Study the habits of successful people to attempt to duplicate the things they did correctly to propel yourself towards your goals.

I first experienced this when I read my first leadership book at the recommendation of a mentor. I was very motivated before I read the book, but the awakening inside me after I completed it changed me forever. I stopped listening to negative influences like rap music or the news. I began replacing those poor role models with productive ones. I took a self-evaluation

106

where I found that most of the information I had been consuming was not productive. I was required to make a life-choice to eliminate it all. My success levels exponentially changed by making these adjustments to the influences I chose to allow into my mind. Yes it was uncomfortable because I had to shut out friends and family who were poor influencers. I had to choose between being successful or following the crowd.

Success will never be found through popular means. True success is found in uncomfortable places where you are challenged. It is found in scary moments when you must make life-changing decisions that others tell you are idiotic. The skill to take advantage of it all is only found through professional development, and in this case it means you must engage in sales training that includes lots of practice.

My favorite activity is to listen to professional development books in my vehicle when I am driving. I average over an hour drive each way when traveling to my clients. I use this time to train. I do not listen to the radio because there is no value in it. Young Jeezy is not going to help me become a millionaire. The low-minded radio personalities only put nonsense into your mind that must be avoided if possible.

I use Google to find the top sales trainers available to learn their content. The most popular today are Grant Cardone, Gary Vaynerchuk, Victor Antonio, Tai Lopez, and Sara Blakely. Studying these success people will allow you to emulate their success. I understand that social media is full of Kardashian posts, rappers, sports celebrities, and other popular people but not positive role models for you as an entrepreneur. You must seek people outside the "popular zone" to find correct roles models to learn from and grow. Do not count the "likes" you see as who to follow. Look at the value they are bringing to you through the positive content they are posting.

I also practice my sales pitch regularly. When I am driving I sometimes turn off my training to do practical exercises. I will go through my entire sales pitch out loud the same as if I was presenting my materials to a customer. These repetitions allow my pitch to be natural when presented. I never stumble over my thoughts because I have practiced it thousands of times. This is the same as the professional baseball player taking thousands of pitches for batting practice, and the more work you put in the better your close rate will become.

Customer Service

Selling your business to others will create a relationship that you will still have to develop to create advocate customers who will promote your business. Your goal should be to create a "WOW experience" for every customer you service. The common sales technique is called "under promise and over deliver".

I do not agree that you should intentionally under promise your customers. My personal philosophy is to give your customers guarantees on your services then provide them with service without deviation. The customers become impressed when you take seemingly commonsense things but deliver them with highly professional consistency. I reward my teams when they maintain a showtime of no later than fifteen minutes earlier than the set appointment time for each customer. I also reward professional appearance, positive reviews received, cleanliness of assigned equipment, and overall customer experience the team members provide.

It is your responsibility to create a culture that rewards excellent customer service. The concept is simple where you deliver first class service to every customer. One of my businesses provides mobile event services to customers. We handle a lot of celebrity events. We treat these people with the same respect we

109

give to anyone else. Our celebrity customers love us because our team respects their privacy. None of our team can blast personal pictures of the events all over their social media. The non-celebrity customers love us because we treat them with the same level of service that the millionaire movie stars or professional athletes receive.

Every customer is valuable. The cost to create a loyal customer can be expensive depending on the competitiveness of your market. The idea is that a customer's value should be three times the cost to acquire them. Your customer service experience will assist in ensuring this number remains low by dealing with customer issues quickly. Selling can sometimes be the easiest part. The best businesses create their successes in customer service.

Costco is one of the best customer service examples. The membership wholesale company works hard to keep their customers happy by delivering the "WOW experience" from all levels of their team. The customer service desk is the focus of their efforts. The culture of the company ensures that every employee stops what they are doing to assist a customer in need. The employees do not care if you are needing help in their department because they understand that customer

110

service is a team effort. If you want to create an amazing customer experience then I recommend you study Costco to adapt some of their philosophies to your business.

Customer service is all about culture for every business. Entrepreneurs are responsible for creating this culture through their personal examples. I was taught that leaders are the first on the battlefield and the last to leave. The concept is that leaders must be involved in the activities of the team to provide the proper example of what is expected. If the leader chooses to not engage in creating the customer service culture creation then the employees will come up with their own versions of what they think is expected. This will lead to a degradation of service where the customer experience will vary depending on who is assisting the customer.

Creating your "WOW experience" requires you to lead your team by example to provide consistency for every customer. Consistency is a trait of success if you are providing consistent 5-star service to all customers. This will create the advocate customer culture that will be the cornerstone of your entrepreneurial venture. Advocate customers are the difference between success and failure because they will sell your business for free while returning to make new purchases. More business will higher revenues and open doors of success for you.

Managing Your Finances

How can millionaire football players become bankrupt within two years of finishing their careers? The idea that a million dollars can run out may seem insane to you. The truth is that if you do a poor job of managing your finances then you could blow through a billion dollars in a short time. Silicon Valley is littered with failed companies who were fed $100 million by investors only to see the money disappear like a magic trick.

Entrepreneurship is sometimes misrepresented by the social media faker culture because they try to show materialistic realities that do not really exist. Pictures are photoshopped to make people appear to be successful, rich, and important when the reality is different. Businesses are now popping up that feeds into this craze where wantrepreneurs can pay to have photoshoots inside private jets, exotic cars, and even makes it look like the faker is on a vacation in an exotic location when none of it is true.

This creates a false perception about what being an entrepreneur is about. Entrepreneurs are people who can identify opportunities then create profitable products

113

or services that fill these market niches. There is nothing flashy about the lifestyle when you are starting. If you are already a billionaire then realistically you are not living the entrepreneur life because you will not endure the choice of personal sacrifice. There is a universal bond between true entrepreneurs because only someone who was sacrificed personal luxuries to invest everything you have into your business can understand the life. I am not saying that you should struggle forever, but there is a period in a new entrepreneur's journey where each one of use looked in the mirror and asked, "why am I doing this?"

What Is A Profit?

Profits are the reason an entrepreneur starts a business. It is the excess revenues your business has after its expenses. Every action you take as an entrepreneur must be directed towards making as much profit as possible.

Profits are many times misunderstood. They are also confused with revenues generated. The revenues you receive from selling your product or service is called "gross profit". This means that it is revenues before expenses have been deducted. After you pay all your bills such as employee wages, vendor payments, maintenance, new equipment purchase, or any other

114

business expense the amount remaining will be the profit.

Profits are usually not very high when you start a venture. The goal is to grow the business by increasing the profits your company makes. Entrepreneurs must constantly evaluate the effectiveness of their processes to ensure there is no waste. Waste is an area where many companies lose profits. This includes the waste of employee time, materials, utilities, or any other business expense. Cutting waste can increase your profit. This creates more capital for you to invest into growing your business.

When Should I Reinvest Capital?

The entrepreneurs that survive are the ones who are fiscally disciplined. That is a fancy way of saying you must manage your business revenues accurately. You cannot waste money on things that are unnecessary. When I mentor other business owners I start by observing their daily processes to figure out if the business is "working for their money" or "letting the money work for them". I prefer to work with entrepreneurs who work hard because I have found that the ones that are trying to make the money work for them have less successes. The reason is because they

115

waste capital paying other people to do tasks they could have just did themselves.

Capital is critical to a new business. Every penny that is spent must be justified and accounted for to ensure your business is set for growth. Most entrepreneurs must forgo being paid for the extreme hours they work in the early periods. The companies that have trouble staying open are usually ones where the entrepreneur starts the business with a set salary being paid to themselves. There are very few businesses that will survive doing this because the capital used personally will cause a deficiency within the budget of the business. When your business is new you must spend higher amounts on customer acquisition. This is the most important place where capital should be spent.

Discipline is required in all areas of the business when it comes to finances. When you start your business you do not need to purchase the newest equipment. You must save money by making decisions on what is the best you can afford. Then over time you can reinvest the capital you earn and upgrade equipment.

I waited over eight years to purchase myself a new truck for my first business. I could have easily diverted funds to paying for a shiny, new truck but instead I used the best one I could afford at that time because I paid cash for it. I reinvested the money I would have spent on a new truck payment into creating my "WOW experience". The best place profits can be reinvested are into areas that will increase the gross profits you make. I always will choose expanding my business instead of paying myself if an opportunity presents itself.

How Do I Pay Myself?

How do I get paid? This is a valid question that many entrepreneurs ask. I recommend that anyone starting a business be willing to fund their personal lives for at least five to seven years because this is an average time it takes for businesses to make a true profit. The milestones of surpassing a year and five years are critical milestones because of the high failure rate of entrepreneurial ventures.

I have already stated that I do not recommend any entrepreneur start a business with them receiving an immediate salary. Entrepreneurs are rewarded by growing a business past the humble salary level to a success that is infinitely bigger. Paying yourself first is selfish because it makes you the focus of the venture. I

117

understand that you must live. I have walked in the shoes you will wear.

When I was starting out I humbly did any odd job I could find. I dressed as an elf to serve rich people hot cocoa. I bartended at night after working my business all day. I sold firewood. I built websites. I trained people on digital marketing. I sold cable to people door-to-door. If I could make money doing it and work around my business schedule then I did it.

I had a jar in my house where I collected all the tips and cash payments. I would pour it all out on the floor at the end of each month to divide it up to pay my bills. I did this all while my new business was making around $30,000 per month. I could have siphoned off profits to pay myself, but I might not have survived the market. I overcame failure when I have seen thirty competitors file bankruptcy.

Three years after starting my first business I built my home. I had finally reached a point where I could make money. It was two years earlier than expected. I had paid the "Law of the Price Tag" and was rewarded with a home I own. This is bigger than a paycheck and should be considered in your journey.

Taxes Are Not Confusing

Taxes are a scary area for many new entrepreneurs. The rules are confusing. The good news is that you do not need to know every detail of tax law to understand how your taxes work.

There are a lot of services for tax preparation to take the burden off you. Tax professionals are a good resource if you have complex tax needs. The average entrepreneur can use the online services like TurboTax. The online services are designed to follow the proper tax procedures for each state and the type of business you operate.

Your responsibility is to know every tax deduction you are authorized. You may have read in the media people complaining about businesses not paying taxes. These misinformed people are referring to the itemized deductible items that is your right to apply to your taxes.

Profits that are not reinvested will be taxed at a high rate. These are lost revenues if you choose to not reinvest these profits. The smart entrepreneur will

119

ensure that all deductions they qualify for are utilized. Reinvesting your capital into new equipment is smarter for your business than donating it to the government.

The best source for understanding the deductions you are allowed is to visit the Internal Revenue Service (IRS) website. It is imperative that you maximize your deductions. You must also always comply with the tax laws that apply to your business. The whole program is not as confusing as it may appear if you take the time to do your research. Everything you need to know is found easily in Google.

Should I Hire Employees

The choice to hire employees should depend on whether you are losing business because you cannot fulfill the needs of your customers. You must evaluate the difference in the loss versus the cost of the new employee. This decision should be decided based on the value of adding another person to your team.

This value should include the understanding that hiring the right person will not increase your productivity by one. When a new person is added that has a strong work ethic their influence will be an exponential increase.

120

Where Do We Go From Here?

When you started reading this book you had an image of entrepreneurship in your mind. You probably picked this book up because you have told yourself or other that you would become the "next Bezos" but you were unsure of how to get there. I hope that your understanding of what it is like to be one has helped grow your desire to join our ranks. You are very capable of creating your own entrepreneurship path if you follow the principles I highlighted in this book. You will be successful if you embrace core values in your business and display discipline in every decision you make.

This book is not just for reading then sitting down. It was written for you to use as a basic guide for the minimum steps required for you to start your own entrepreneurial venture. The information is not the end of the road if you want to be successful you will be required to be a student of your craft to continually learn new concepts about being successful in your business. There are thousands of books on each subject highlighted in the table of contents of this book. I am also writing more books on the individual steps I highlighted in this book to compliment these basic lessons. Use it as a guide for researching the information that you require to improve.

Do not feel like you must know everything when you start your venture. No matter how experienced you are in business you will find that each new venture will create its own set of challenges. You cannot use a "cookie-cutter approach" to be successful because of the diversity of each venture. You can adapt a foundation of core values, consistent work ethic, and effective time management as positive traits that you employ to complete all tasks required to reach your desired results for every aspect of your business.

You must remember that business successes are never immediate. The average "overnight success" people rave about will usually be traceable back many years where the entrepreneur fought through adversity to break all the barriers standing in the way of their success. The time it takes to reach your full operations potential will vary of many factors so it is important to approach your overall business by segmenting the parts into smaller, manageable pieces that you can create action plans to complete those specific goals.

The old saying goes, "to eat an elephant you must take one bite at a time." This applies to entrepreneurial ventures well because you will be juggling many tasks at once requiring you to identify all tasks by priority. I always do any task that makes money immediately first. It is because this is the primary purpose of a business. If you do not make money then having the perfect logo, creating the most efficient process, or hiring the perfect team member does not matter if you do not produce enough revenues to pay the bills.

I also believe that you should not allow yourself to become bogged down in the details of every piece of your business. When you are starting out momentum is the most important thing you must create. You do not need perfection at this point, you need revenues, and you must take massive actions on those tasks at that point. Create the best website you can do now then work on it in between money making tasks. I find many wantrepreneurs stuck chasing perfection their entire lives resulting in nothing being accomplished.

Get moving now. Get revenues now. That is your mission to start. Do not worry about having the perfect advertisement to mail out to your target market. I have made hundreds of thousands of dollars using handwritten mailers because I did not have enough money when I started to buy the supplies to make nicer ones. I found getting the message out was more important than having the perfect flyer. A perfect advertisement sitting on your desktop will never make you money. Get the creatives done and get them in customer hands. That is the most effective process. You can hire design teams that make perfect ads when you are a billionaire, but for now get it moving.

Your most important step is to start acting on your vision of what you have created. If you want to be the next Bezos then it will take massive actions daily. You must refocus your daily habits to attack your dream with tangible actions. Remember the namesake for this culture started in a garage before he dominated the retail space and before he put historically "too big to fail" retailers out of business. He was able to do this because while they hosted meetings to discuss other meetings he was building a dominate space online where the giants paid little attention.

The next Bezos will come from an industry that is not paying attention making it perfect for a hostile takeover. Look around your current market to see the opportunities that are low-hanging fruit to pick off then go for it. My philosophy is to find the opportunity then run as fast as you can towards it until you are so far ahead of your peers that they can never catch you. This is what the next Bezos will be required to do. Are your ready to dominate? Then run now!

124

Acknowledgments

This book was written for all the people who have that feeling like there is something bigger out there for them. I hope this book can be a guide for you to start your journey. Every story of success started with an idea that someone put action behind it. If you want to be the next Bezos then today is the day. Stop talking. Get to work.

The difference in successful people and everyone else is the former did not stop at the idea. They had a thought then took curiosity in it to the point where people now know their names. There would be no Apple without Steve Jobs because Steve Wozniak was content with making the computer boards as a hobby. Wozniak had created something amazing that never would have been known to the world if not for the passion Jobs had for making the product amazing.

There is no reason to give up on your dreams just because you are comfortable, established, or even lazy. You can become an entrepreneur if you are 7 years old or 70. The decision is yours to make. If you have that pull then follow the steps in this book to get your idea into a tangible form. After that enjoy the ride!

About the Author

Ellis Franks

Ellis Franks has dedicated his life to helping top performers achieve the highest levels of personal and team performance. He is an avid student of leadership personally mentoring over 3,000 performers to reach their full potential. His experience has been obtained from over 14 years as a military leader, top performer, and led to his selection to special duties open to only 1percent of the total 350,000 active members. He earned some of the highest performance awards attainable personal performance. He was honored to have received personal mentorship time with all the living Chief Master Sergeants of the Air Force, multiple Secretary of the Air Force & Under-Secretary of the Air Force, and numerous other high-ranking leaders during his career.

His military experience includes over 5,000 platform teaching hours in various subjects to include Anti-Terrorism Force Protection, Combat First Aid Skills, and Basic Military Training Instructor Trainer. He began his journey as a leader teaching basic training recruits the skills needed to become excellent team members and future leaders. He excelled at the mentorship of his troops by incorporating the lessons of John C. Maxwell's "21 Irrefutable Laws of Leadership" & " 17 Indisputable Laws of Teamwork" into every

126

lesson he taught. He directly impacted the lives of thousands of new Airmen, many of which continually contact him to say thanks for changing their lives.

Ellis has continued to excel in the civilian market pursuing numerous entrepreneurial opportunities to include starting new markets from concept, creating nation's largest adventure sports brokerage firms, launching digital advertising start-ups, and numerous sales consulting ventures. He has created highly skilled sales and marketing teams for numerous industries including inbound call centers & door-to-door direct marketing teams culminating in millions of dollars in sales for multiple industries. His secret to success is providing core value-based sales approach to his clients by always following the three core values that were ingrained within him in the US Air Force - *Integrity First, Service Before Self, & Excellence In All You Do.*

Now his career has come full circle to pass on the knowledge he has developed over a 25-year career in leadership, team building, and business. He believes anyone can become a self-made success by always displaying a high energy level and refusing to accept mediocrity in any form. These traits paired with the foundational training from the top leadership and sales mentors in their perspective industries are the basis for all training programs that have been developed to make your team the best in your industry.

AWARDS & RECOGNITION

- Published Author: "The Next Bezos"

- Published Author: "Always Leave An Airman Behind"

- Certified John C. Maxwell Leadership Coach February 2016

- Certified Google Partner July 2012

- Selected as CEO largest adventure sports network in the world—10K websites nationally & $40M revenues

- Created Game Cave Atlanta—successfully hosted over 6,000 events in metro Atlanta September 2011

- Recognized #1 Salesperson Video Game Truck Sales in US -Volume & Per Unit Sales May 2011

- 2010 Kuk Sool Won World Championships Bronze Medalist (3 medals total)

- Founded Kuk Sool Won of Bagram, Afghanistan (Non-Profit) June 2010

- Co-Founded Zepol Optimized December 2009

- 2009 Kuk Sool Won European Champion Medalist & 3rd Place Team—4 medals total

- 2008 Air Force Sergeants Association International Member of the Year

- 2008 United States Air Force Warren R. Carter Daedalian Silver Award—European Command winner

•2008 Air Force Sergeants Association Division 16 (Europe) Member of the Year

•2008 Air Force Sergeants Association Chapter 1669 (Royal Air Forces Lakenheath) Member of the Year

•2008 Kuk Sool Won European Championship School & Gold Medalist

•2008 Kuk Sool Won United Kingdom Championship School & Gold Medalist

•2008 Kuk Sool Won Scottish Champion Gold Medalist

•Graduated Air Force Senior Non-Commissioned Officer Academy (Strategic Leadership) Aug 2008

•2007 Kuk Sool Won European Championship School & Gold Medalist

•2007 Kuk Sool Won United Kingdom Championship School & Gold Medalist

•2007 Kuk Sool Won Spanish Champion Gold Medalist

•2007 American Petroleum Institute Fuels Management Silver Award

•2007 United States Air Forces in Europe Golden Drum Winner--Best in European Command

•2007 Air Force Sergeants Association NCO of the Year International Finalist

•2007 Air Force Sergeants Association Division 16 (Europe) NCO of the Year

•2007 Mission Support Group Team of the Year

•2007 Fuels Management Flight NCO of the Year

•Kisling Non-Commissioned Officer Academy Distinguished Graduate May 2007

•Mission Support Group Team of the Quarter Jan-Mar 2007

•48th Logistics Readiness Squadron NCO of the Quarter Jul-Sep 2007

•Air Force Commendation Medal 2006 (Meritorious Service)

•Selected Special Duty: US Air Force Special Tactics, Combat Controller

•Certified DoD Anti-Terrorism Officer October 2004

•Earned Military Training Instructor "Black Rope" (Instructor Mentor & Trainer) September 2004

•Selected Air Force Active Duty Baseball Team— competed nationally against NCAA teams (4-year starter)

•Military Training Instructor School Distinguished Graduate May 2002

•Selected Special Duty: Military Training Instructor

•347th Supply Squadron NCO of the Quarter Apr-Jun & Jul-Aug 2001

•Navy Commendation Letter 2001 (Operation Southern Watch)

•Air Force Achievement Medal 2001 (Operation Southern Watch)

•Air Force Achievement Medal 1999 (Meritorious Service - Korean Defense Campaign)

•Air Force Achievement Medal 1998 (Meritorious Service)

•1997 Supply Squadron Eagle Leadership Award

•1997 Fuels Management Flight Airman of the Year

•Selected 37th Fighter Wing Honor Guard Jan 1997

•1996 Fuels Management Academic Achievement of the Year

•37th Fuels Management Flight Airman of the Quarter Apr-Jun, July-Sep, & Oct-Dec 1996

•347th Supply Squadron NCO of the Quarter Apr-Jun & Jul-Aug 2001

•Navy Commendation Letter 2001 (Operation Southern Watch)

•Air Force Achievement Medal 2001 (Operation Southern Watch)

•Air Force Achievement Medal 1999

•Air Force Achievement Medal 1998

•1997 Supply Squadron Eagle Leadership Award

•1997 Fuels Management Flight Airman of the Year

•1996 Fuels Management Academic Achievement of the Year

"Everyone talks about being successful,

Entrepreneurs take massive actions to make it a reality"

- **Ellis Franks**